The Great Comeback from Domestic Violence

Cheryl L. Gebbie

ISBN: 9798852902153

DEDICATION

This book is dedicated to those that are currently in a domestic violence relationship of any kind, as well as those that are survivors and the ones that are completely and totally **Healed**.

ACKNOWLEDGMENTS

I would like to acknowledge for and foremost GOD. Because if it were not for my Lord and Savior, I would have never made it out and be totally healed from this ordeal. Secondly, I would like to thank my daughter Rebecca Smith for placing the Write a book bug in my ears many years ago. Then I want to thank Sherry Lavon Williams of the Sols Write House and She Will Heal Ministry for abiding to what God was leading her to give me a leg up and helping me build my self-confidence up and to Find my Boldness to speak up about Domestic Violence and the POWER GOD gives us because Healed People really do HEAL People Last but definitely not Least I want to Acknowledge Apostle Jerry Upton of Honey Rock Victorious Church International that allowed The SOLs Write House and She Will Heal Ministry

The Great Comeback from Domestic Violence

CONTENTS

Domestic Violence
Hotline 800-799-7233
SMS: text START TO
88788

1 WHAT IS DOMESTIC VIOLENCE

Domestic violence is violence committed by someone in the victim's domestic circle of family and friends. This includes partners and ex-partners, immediate family members, other relatives, and family friends. The term 'domestic violence' is used when there is a close relationship between the offender and the victim.

I am going to give you some of the most recent facts about domestic violence from the National Coalition Against Domestic Violence:

- On average, almost 20 million people (about the population of New York) per minute are physically abused by an intimate partner in the United States. For one year, this equates to more than 10 million women (about half the population of New York) and men.

- 1 in 4 women and 1 in 9 men experience severe intimate partner physical violence, intimate partner contact, sexual violence, and/or intimate partner stalking with impacts such as injury, fearfulness, post-traumatic stress disorder, use of victim services, contraction of sexually transmitted diseases, etc.
- 1 in 3 women and 1 in 4 men have experienced some form of physical violence by an intimate partner. This includes a range of behaviors (e.g., slapping, shoving, pushing) and in some cases might not be considered "domestic violence."
- 1 in 7 women and 1 in 25 men have been injured by an intimate partner.
- 1 in 10 women have been raped by an intimate partner. Data is unavailable on male victims.

- 1 in 4 women and 1 in 7 men have been victims of severe physical violence (e.g., beating, burning, strangling) by an intimate partner in their lifetime.
- 1 in 7 women and 1 in 18 men have been stalked by an intimate partner during their lifetime to the point in which they felt very fearful or believed that they or someone close to them would be harmed or killed.
- On a typical day, there are more than 20,000 phone calls placed to domestic violence hotlines nationwide.

- The presence of a gun in domestic violence situations increases the risk of homicide by 500%.
- Intimate partner violence accounts for 15% of all violent crime.

- Women between the ages of 18-24 are most abused by an intimate partner.
- 19% of domestic violence involves a weapon.
- Domestic victimization is correlated with a higher rate of depression and suicidal behavior.
- Only 34% of people who are injured by intimate partners receive medical care for their injuries.

RAPE

- 1 in 5 women and 1 in 71 men in the United States has been raped in their lifetime.

- Almost half of female (46.7%) and male (44.9%) victims of rape in the United States were raped by an acquaintance. Of these, 45.4% of female rape victims and 29% of male rape victims were raped by an intimate partner.

STALKING

- 19.3 million women (about the population of New York) and 5.1 million men (about twice the population of Mississippi) in the United States have been stalked in their lifetime. 60.8% of female stalking victims and 43.5% men reported being stalked by a current or former intimate partner.

HOMICIDE

- A study of intimate partner homicides found that 20% of victims were not the intimate partners themselves, but family members, friends, neighbors, persons who intervened, law enforcement responders, or bystanders.
- 72% of all murder-suicides involve an intimate partner; 94% of the victims of these murder suicides are female.

CHILDREN AND DOMESTIC VIOLENCE

- 1 in 15 children are exposed to intimate partner violence each year, and 90% of these children are eyewitnesses to this violence.

ECONOMIC IMPACT

- Victims of intimate partner violence lose a total of 8.0 million days (about 21903 years) of paid work each year.
- The cost of intimate partner violence exceeds $8.3 billion (about $26 per person in the US) per year.
- Between 21-60% of victims of intimate partner violence lose their jobs due to reasons stemming from the abuse.
- Between 2003 and 2008, 142 women were murdered in their workplace by their abuser, 78% of women killed in the workplace during this period.

PHYSICAL/MENTAL IMPACT

- Women abused by their intimate partners are more vulnerable to contracting HIV or other STI's due to forced intercourse or prolonged exposure to stress.
  - Studies suggest that there is a relationship between intimate partner violence and depression and suicidal behavior.
  - Physical, mental, and sexual and reproductive health effects have been linked with intimate partner violence including adolescent pregnancy, unintended pregnancy in general, miscarriage, stillbirth, intrauterine hemorrhage, nutritional deficiency, abdominal pain and other gastrointestinal problems, neurological disorders, chronic pain, disability, anxiety, and post-

traumatic stress disorder (PTSD), as well as noncommunicable diseases such as hypertension, cancer, and cardiovascular diseases. Victims of domestic violence

- The cost of intimate partner violence exceeds $8.3 billion (about $26 per person in the US) per year.
- Between 21-60% of victims of intimate partner violence lose their jobs due to reasons stemming from the abuse.
- Between 2003 and 2008, 142 women were murdered in their workplace by their abuser, 78% of women killed in the workplace during this period.

Notes

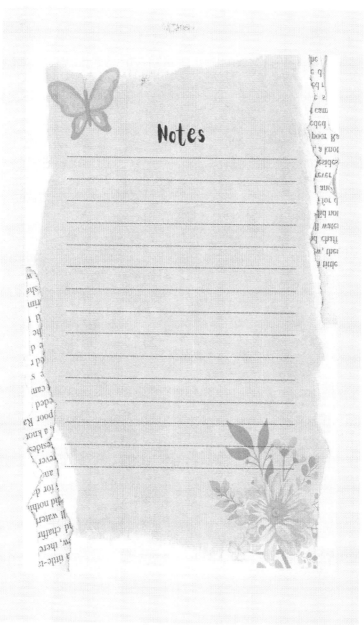

Notes

Notes

2. How I Got into This Relationship

You may ask how someone might get involved up in a relationship or marriage involving domestic violence. Well, I do not know how others did, but I sure know how it happened to me. My Story begins when I was just 16 yrs. old. In the Summer of 1978. It was so exciting because it was not till the age of sixteen, I was FINALLY allowed to date. It was a crazy summer. Getting my very first job and started dating and even lost weight so I was so heavy as I was in my previous year of school. I was working at the Ponderosa Steak House busing tables and one day this guy came in who worked for the florist that took care of the plants in the restaurant. He would always say hello and ask me how I was doing just a little chit chat. I knew he was older because he was not a student at my high school SO, WOW an older guy seemed to like me.

But also, during this time My sister Ro along with a Neighbor and myself got together and formed a trio where on the weekends we would travel locally to church for homecomings and picnics to sing for them. And I was not really looking for a boyfriend of sorts because we were too busy. Meanwhile at the restaurant my ex would show up every day to water the plants and make small talk with me. He was so nice, or so I thought.

Turned out David was 18 yrs. old to my 16 was more mature than any of the guys I went to school with. I really started to like him. It was getting later in the summer, and he asked me to go out with him. But I told him he would have to meet my mom first. Well, we lived out toward the country, and he lived in town with no car so to meet my mom he hitchhiked all the way to my house, much to my surprise. I had never known anyone that would hitchhike. He must have REALLY liked me. Mom did not really care for him, but she did allow us to go out and for him to come visit. And soon I found myself falling in love, at least that is what I thought love felt like. It is hard for a young girl to really know what love looks like between a man and woman when you grew up in a single parent home and your dad passed away when your 6 yrs.

old. Little did I know that jealousy is not really a sign of love, it is a kind of signal that should warn ladies to watch out!

David started sharing increasingly more about his family. His mom and dad and that he had six brothers not including himself. He would talk about things they would do as a family and later even talked about the abuse his mom endured at his father's hands. Even the abuse the sons received growing up. I had never heard of a man hitting a woman or child. I was instructed men do not hit women or kids and here I am hearing about the violence in this family and all I wanted to do was make things better for him. I sure did not know at that point I would end up being one of those abused women. In the meantime, how could someone like me with no father figure growing up know how to help a man overcome the abuse he received most of his life.

We dated all year that year and in June of 1979 I found out I was pregnant. We got married in July and at that point he had no idea how he would support his small family with the small job he had been working just to support himself. One day he came home and said let me know he had enlisted into the Army and would be leaving for bootcamp at the end of the week.

We lived separately the better part the first two years of our marriage first Bootcamp then his training and then on to GERMANY. When he got back from Germany, he had one more year in the military and he was stationed at Ft Bliss in El Paso Texas. It was while in El Paso I got my first taste of domestic violence. This is where it truly began.

We did good for a while then one day he started to drink, he drank an extreme about that day, more than I had ever seen him drink. I cannot remember what It was I was supposed to do for him but whatever it was I did not do it the way he wanted. First the yelling, then the slapping and then the punch in the eye.

My eye no longer had white around the pupil. It was red from where the blood vessel burst. The next morning while he was at work, I grabbed our daughter and a few things, called my mom who got me a bus ticket back home. Only one problem, I had no transportation. So, we started walking and I just knew that we were going to miss the bus … I was carrying my oldest daughter Becky in one arm and a bag with clothes in with the other and began walking and asking for directions to the Greyhound bus station. Someone finally felt pity for use and drove us to the station where we got on the bus and headed home. I did not have money for food for Becky or myself or for water and milk, but GOD made sure we had even just a little to get us by.

We finally got home and the next day I got the first phone call from my ex wanting us to come back and he was sorry and that he would never do that again. Here I am thinking How am I supposed to care for a baby by myself at 19 yrs. of age. His mom got the money together and. Got us a ticket to go back to TX and this time we had extra so could eat and drinks without handouts. The rest of that year he was on his best behavior. I got pregnant with my second child while I was in Texas. And almost had an abortion but after paying for it I could not go through with it, and I praise GOD for that every day.

This my friends this is how I GOT INTO THE CYCLE OF DOMESTIC VIOLENCE

It was not long from the time he got out of the service that we moved back to WV and a few months later I had my son Joshua.

We had our own apartment, but work was exceedingly rare if you did not know someone you could not get a job. So, David moved to Kannapolis NC where his brother and his wife were living and working and got a job in the Canon Mills Textile Mill. And soon came and his small family and moved us down to North Carolina with him.

It did not take time for the abuse to begin again, and this time became increasingly intense. What is bad though is there is really no way to predict when he would wake up in a bad mood or good mood and North Carolina was the beginning of the NEW season of pain and suffering at the hands of the man that was supposed to love me and never hurt me, 20+ yrs. not knowing then it was going to happen. 20 yrs. of being on pins and needles.

Notes

Notes

Notes

3. What Happened

Some may ask, "what do you mean about The Start of New Beginning?" For most people that is a positive thing in their lives. For me it was my Nightmare when he was not working. This is where domestic violence kicked into high gear using all forms of aggressive forms and manners. Some examples included Kicking, punching, forcing me to smoke marijuana, shoving me in the corner behind the bed and throwing all the pillows and covers over me and dare me to say anything or move. This led to claustrophobia.

This started out with just the yelling and name calling me, the accusations of cheating. All the time thinking to myself, "what I have done to deserve this. I am just 21 yrs. old. The only thing I could think of why this happened was it was my

punishment for having premarital sex."
God was punishing me for disobeying
him. Why else would this be happening
to me? I had never seen any man treat this
wife this way .so it had to be something I
caused, and David reinforced this
thought. He said, "If you had not done
this or if you had done exactly what I told
you I would not have hurt you. IF you
had not been embarrassed me by looking
at that man walking down the road on the
other side of the road, I would not have
been forced to do this or that. Why do
you want to go to Church so much? Are
you having sex with the preacher? Then
that punching. Then I was a slut or a
whore. The beatings and kicks would get
worse from this point. During this time,
his brother was living with us, and he was
sleeping around with my friend. This day,
he accused me of sleeping with the
brother as well and he kicked me down,
beat me and called me a name. ended up

with bruised bones and could barely move. After this incident, he would allow me to get a job. However, after a few months he would start the accusations and make me quit. It was during one of the times I was working that he got extremely mad. Again, I was accused of being unfaithful. This time he beat me in the face (all the other times the bruises were in places that could not be seen. During the night when the kids were sleeping, he would continue hitting me, punching me, and kicking and prodded me with a stick. He would not even let me go to the bathroom without him coming in with me to make sure I did not leave. He would not allow me to sleep, and he did not sleep for fear I would call the police. He would not give me any privacy that night and like said even to go to the bathroom he would go with me. Soon the kids woke up to get ready for school. He allowed me to get them ready for school and we drove them to school to keep other parents at the bus stop from seeing me. After the kids were in school, he started apologizing. Which never lasted long. He calmed down after this and things got better for the time being.

I finally got the nerve to let him know I was leaving him and much to my surprise he was agreeable. A few weeks after the separation started, he would start coming to see the kids and would begin the accusations again and name calling. This time he would start calling my mom to get her involved. Giving her a sob story every time. At one point she came to get the kids so we could talk things out and try to work out our problems. He had her believe it was me.

You see through these past 7 yrs. I would leave and go back. I would give it to GOD and then think I cannot make it on my own with three children. I would pick it back up from the foot of the Cross and Go Back over and over. All the while he was begging me to come back, and he was manipulating my mom in believing it was my fault. This time the kids went to moms in WV, and I had gone to see a friend down the street. When I got home, he was waiting for me, and the violence started again. The yelling the hitting, punching, and shoving me down. This time when he shoved me, I was not able to get back up. My leg was shattered. He got scared and took me to the Emergency Room all the time, beginning with me to tell them he did it. However, when I went in the back and going to Xray I told him to not let him near me and that he did this to me. At this point, the Police were called. My leg was shattered and was in a cast for 3 months. Six weeks no weight bearing. I was living with my mom during the healing process. I applied for

Subsidized housing and not long after that He moved back to our hometown as well… I had gotten my divorce before he moved back. When he got back, he would visit the kids and beg me to marry him again. I kept saying no till my mom accused me of sleeping with him and she was going to report me to the state because my welfare check was based on him not being in the house. In my anger at mom, I agreed to remarry him. He was being good, and we got remarried and then moved to Kentucky for me to go to college at then named Cumberland College now named University of the Cumberlands in the Fall of 1992. During these 4 yrs. he would yell some, but he never hit me. We had some good times in Kentucky.

After I graduated in the Spring of 1996 we moved to Kansas City, MO to be close to my sister and her husband. We lived with them till we found jobs and a place to live. We even got along decently that year as well. My sister and husband were moving to California, so our family moved to Johnson City, TN... Things started again in Johnson City. This time he would not only yell at me but the kids as well. And threatening them. It was after he informed me that he was paying for our youngest child's lunch at church, but I had to reimburse him for the other two's lunches. And I was already paying the rent and utilities. I had to get away and so I took the kids and went to moms for the weekend. Much to my dislike, He made the trip after he got off work and we were gone. Suddenly he rapidly pulls into the driveway in front of mom's house. Again, all apologetic and I just told him I am done but he needed help. He agreed to let me drive him back to Johnson City that night and go to the VA to get help and that they did. All was

good and he was admitted into one of
their programs and all was good. I would
take the kids to visit him and even take
him snacks and things. Then ONE DAY
he came to my job to bring flowers and to
let me know he had gotten a job and
needed to get his welding equipment
from my apartment. I said it would, He
would have to wait till Sunday be we had
a youth event at the church that evening
and I would not be home for him to get
his stuff. Later that Saturday evening he
shows up at church wanting my
apartment key to get his stuff. I said NO
but to keep things quiet at church I had
someone bring the kids home after the
service and I went to let him in. the whole
time throwing out the accusations again
and calling me names. When the kids
arrived, he started on our son. His GF
was with him, and he would call him
names and accused him of being gay in
front of his Girl Friend. The next day he

came back to my work and was coming to the office floor when he was stopped by management and informed, he could not be there and that they would send me out… Thanks to the management for watching because as he was leaving, he drove the car toward me and was going to hit me.

ANYWAY, I digress. After he got his stuff, he forgot the welding stuff so that evening I dropped it off at the VA without letting him visit the kids. I did not know that he was in the part of the program that he was giving his meds to himself…thing was he was not taking them. The gentleman at the front desk there took the welding equipment to him. a few minutes later while at him. He comes flying into the complex. He busted into my home and threatened me. Our son ran out the back door and called the police. It was just a few minutes before they showed up and there was a standoff. He was throwing my stuff at the police and broke my stereo and tv at this point the police officers realized the back door was open from when my son went out … I was able to get out the back door and the police came in and took him down.

I WAS FINALLY OUT!

The Great Comeback from Domestic Violence

Notes

Notes

4. The Great Comeback

As stated, At the end of the last chapter I was free from abuse, however. I was not free mentally. All the hidden memories and anxieties and depression hit me hard, with a harsh swoop. My job ended and due to no longer being in a marriage, my landlord rented the apartment out from underneath me. Little did he know that it was me that had been paying the rent the whole time, unsure what to do. My sisters in Christ helped me get into a public housing Which looking back, was not a promising idea. My depression got worse, at a time when my three children needed me most, I was hard to keep the house clean, to cook the meals. It was hard for me to do much of anything. I got lax on things like applying for food stamps, keeping the office updated on what I was doing to find work. I was still attending church, but it was more out of habit than anything else. It was during this time of discovered online group chat. Which was good and bad, led to several years of living my life online and not in the real world. However, I still love God, but I was confused, hurt, and lost.

It was during this time I met Kevin, who ended up being my best friend online, and he only lived two hours away from me.

We decided he was going to visit me, take me to breakfast, when he showed up. I thought, what have I gotten myself into? I never was one that judged a book by its cover, so I set aside the fact that he did not wear his dentures except for when he was eating. This fact was on. This fact was an inside joke between the two of us. It was that day we drove to Mountain City TN. There was a lake that was gorgeous, surrounded by mountains. We walked around and we talked and held hands. God said to him at that time. "You have been praying for Her, here she is. Do not lose her. And he said to me, "It is time for me to be happy and safe.

Kevin had been actively looking and praying for someone. He had never been married, but he did not want to leave the rest of his life alone because he had been sick. And he been searching, searching, and searching, and God led him to me, and me to him. He drove me home, met the kids too good for ice cream, and he traveled back to Maxville because he had worked that night. The next few days we talked for hours each day. And a friend lent me her car to visit Knoxville. Next morning, he asked me to marry him. This was close to a year since the separation from the abuser and two months from the divorce. I agreed to marry him. It was just two weeks later my job ended, Unsure how I was going to pay my bills. Kevin said since we are getting married just move down here, I will help with the kids. Will work different shifts and I already have a home. About 2 weeks later we are going to Knoxville. 2 months later we got married at the courthouse. But we had a Faux Ceremony in August. During the ceremony God Revealed to me the same thing he had spoken to

Kevin, you needed stability and you needed someone to show you true love here he is, enjoy your life. We were married 12 years and 1 day he passed away. This was hard because my son was killed a few years earlier on the job in 2009, and I blamed God for his passing as stated earlier in this book. Before Kevin passed away. He asked One thing, He asked would I go back to church. Josh's death was not God's fault. Things just happen. And because of that, I went back to church. A few years later God led me to Honey Rock Victorious Church International in Knoxville, TN. This is where my real healing started. This is where God said the pain has lasted long enough, even though you covered it up. And you think you were healed. Now it is

time to truly be healed by letting go. The
key was giving forgiveness. The Holy
Spirit came into me and released the
unforgiveness to my abuser. I felt like I
was walking on clouds when the Spirit
filled me that day with forgiveness. But
little did I know the next Sunday God
said I need you to release Forgiveness to
one more person. This person was my
granddaughter's dad. I blamed him the
death of my son. He is that person that
said the last time he said to my son. I
hope you get killed while you are driving
down the road in your truck. A few days
later, my son was dead. And I had to
forgive him. I had to let go. My true
healing began with the guidance of
Honey Rock Victorious Church
International. I started learning to trust

God, how to study the word of God. How to prepare my heart for praise, how to worship my not just with words, but with my heart, I learned that I am truly a child of the One True Living God, and I have learned that wherever I am I need God. Whatever I am doing I need God. All Things are possible if we ask in the powerful name of Jesus.

God placed a few people in my life, but one person who he wanted her to take me and teach me my voice. Teach me how to be bold in my faith. How to use my stories to help others survive. Sherry Lavon Williams thank you for allowing God to work through you to bring me out of my shell. Now working with two wonderful ministries: She Will Heal Ministry Directed. By Sherry Lavon

Williams and t

To blessed 2 be stressed Ministry directed by Marla Higginbotham Ladies, I love you both very much for everything you are allowing God to do in your lives and allowing me to serve with both of you. In the She Will Heal ministry, our motto is, Healed People – Heal People. This ministry led me to work with. The To Blessed 2 Be Stressed Ministry Thank you God for allowing me to work with these two great ministries.

Notes

Notes

5. How Can You Get out and Be Healed

It is easy getting out of domestic violence relationship, but we deserve to not live in fear. You will hear people say, why doesn't she just leave? That is the question in people's minds. We know it is not that easy. You have been forced to alienate your family; it is even harder. Things come to our mind like I cannot call my family because I have shut them out for so long. They will be mad at me, and we will help. What we as the victims and survivors do not realize is that most families know the reason behind the isolation. Most of the time our families and friends are just waiting for you or me to make the first call to them. Mama, can you pick me up and the kids up? I cannot go through this anymore. Our loved ones will jump at the chance to assist us. Something that most do not realize is the danger and that you and that person can be in so be careful, its best to do this when the abuser is nowhere around if you can. If you cannot contact authorities to assist you even if it means scheduling time with them. Well, I finally got out. I had to let God take over, let him have the control, because I knew I could not do it alone. I learned that I could not, give it to God one day, two days later, pick it back up and go back. Go back to the abuser to many times I had done this, take it to the cross and go pick it back from the cross and carry it myself. That is not how you get healed. It was at this point in my life. I gave it all to him like that till the cross

and walked away for good. It was after
this God started working in my life but
the one thing, I just started learning was
made to heal completely and totally. They
had to learn to forgive. Not only
forgiving my abuser, truly, but to forgive
myself for allowing myself to feel that I
did not deserve any better. This feel this
is the hardest forgiveness I have ever
given to anyone but necessary. to Quote
Amelia Love who is the author along
with a few of her friends who authored
the book "How to B Happy."
"Forgiveness is one of the most important
words in the human language. It is very
important for you to know what
happiness is Not. Forgiveness does not
mean that what they say or do is OK.
Forgiveness does not mean you are

letting them off the hook. Forgiveness does not mean that you have. To connect with them. It is simply to remove the toxic emotions." This knowledge gave me peace in knowing I am not helping him by forgiving him, but empowering myself to the understand that forgiveness gives me freedom to grow and become who God. One last thing I have found out with God part of your healing process, one can never completely be healed.

The Great Comeback from Domestic Violence

61

Notes

6. Extra Information on Domestic Violence Month in October

This is just some extra information that I located on the riseaboveviolence.org website:

Domestic Violence Awareness Month (DVAM) evolved from the "Day of Unity" held in October 1981 and conceived by the National Coalition Against Domestic Violence. The intent was to connect advocates across the nation who were working to end violence against women and their children.

The Day of Unity soon became an entire week devoted to a range of activities conducted at the local, state, and national level. The activities conducted were as varied and diverse as the program sponsors but had common themes:

- Mourning those who have died because of domestic violence.
- Celebrating those who have survived.
- Connecting those who work to end violence.

These three themes remain a key focus of DVAM events today.

In October 1987, the first Domestic Violence Awareness Month was observed. That same year marks the initiation of the first national domestic violence toll-free hotline.

In 1989, the U.S. Congress passed Public Law 101-112 designating October of that year as *National Domestic Violence Awareness Month*. Such legislation has passed every year since with the National

Coalition Against Domestic Violence providing key leadership in this effort. Each year, the Day of Unity is celebrated on the first Monday of Domestic Violence Awareness Month.

Notes

Notes

Notes

Notes

_____
_____
_____
_____
_____
_____
_____
_____
_____
_____
_____
_____
_____

7. Resources

The Resources listed below were obtained from the National Domestic Hot Line Website.

https://www.thehotline.org/get-help/domestic-violence-local-resources/

Alabama Coalition Against Domestic Violence
Hotline: 1-800-650-6522

Email: info@acadv.org

Website: **http://www.acadv.org/**

Alaska Network on Domestic Violence & Sexual Assault
Office: 907-586-3650

Email: andvsa@andvsa.org

Website: **https://andvsa.org/**
Arizona Coalition To End Sexual & Domestic Violence
Hotline: 1-800-782-6400

Email: helpline@acesdv.org

Website: **https://www.acesdv.org/**

Arkansas Coalition Against Domestic Violence
Hotline: 1-800-269-4668

Email: info@domesticpeace.com

Website: **https://www.domesticpeace.com/**
California Partnership to End Domestic Violence
Office: 916-444-7163

Email: info@cpedv.org

Website: **https://www.cpedv.org/**
Violence Free Colorado
Office: 303-831-9632

Email: info@violencefreeco.org

Website: **https://www.violencefreecolorado.org/**
Connecticut Coalition Against Domestic Violence
Hotline: 1-888-774-2900

Email: contactus@ctcadv.org

Website: **http://www.ctcadv.org/**
Delaware Coalition Against Domestic Violence
Office: 302-658-2958

Website: **https://dcadv.org/**
DC Coalition Against Domestic Violence

Office: 202-299-1181

Email: info@dccadv.org

Website: **https://dccadv.org/**
Florida Department of Children and Families
Hotline: (800) 500-1119

Website: **https://www.myflfamilies.com /service-programs/domestic- violence/map.shtml**
Georgia Coalition Against Domestic Violence
Hotline: 1 (800) 334-2836

Website: **www.gcadv.org**
Guam Coalition Against Sexual Assault & Family Violence
Office: (671) 479-2277

Email: info@guamcoalition.org

Website: **www.guamcoalition.org**
Hawaii State Coalition Against Domestic Violence
Office: (808) 832-9316

Website: **www.hscadv.org**
Idaho Coalition Against Sexual & Domestic Violence
Office: (208) 384-0419

Email: info@engagingvoices.org

Website: **www.idvsa.org**
Illinois Coalition Against Domestic Violence
Hotline: (877) 863-6338

Website: **www.ilcadv.org**
Indiana Coalition Against Domestic Violence
Hotline: 1 (800) 332-7385

Website: **www.icadvinc.org**

Iowa Coalition against Domestic Violence
Hotline: 1 (800) 942-0333

Email: icadv@icadv.org

Website: **www.icadv.org**
Kansas Coalition against Sexual & Domestic
Violence
Hotline: 1 (888) 363-2287

Website: **www.kcsdv.org**
Kentucky Coalition Against Domestic Violence
Office: 502-209-5382

Email: info@kcadv.org

Website: **https://kcadv.org/index.php**
Louisiana Coalition Against Domestic Violence
Hotline: 1 (888) 411-1333

Website: **www.lcadv.org**

Maine Coalition to End Domestic Violence
Hotline: 1 (866) 834-4357

Email: info@mcedv.org

Website: **www.mcedv.org**
Maryland Network Against Domestic Violence
Hotline: 1 (800) 634-3577

Email: info@mnadv.org

Website: **www.mnadv.org**
Massachusetts Coalition Against Sexual Assault &
Domestic Violence / Jane Doe, Inc.
Hotline: 1 (877) 785-2020

Email: info@janedoe.org

Website: **www.janedoe.org**
Michigan Coalition To End Domestic & Sexual
Violence
Office: (517) 347-7000

Website: **www.mcedsv.org**
Violence Free Minnesota
Hotline: 1 (866) 223-1111

Website: **https://www.vfmn.org/**
Mississippi Coalition Against Domestic Violence
Hotline: 1 (800) 898-3234

Email: support@mcadv.org

Website: **www.mcadv.org**
Missouri Coalition Against Domestic & Sexual Violence
Office: (573) 634-4161

Website: **www.mocadsv.org**
Montana Coalition Against Domestic & Sexual Violence
Office: (406) 443-7794

Email: mtcoalition@mcadsv.com

Website: **www.mcadsv.com**
Nebraska Coalition to End Sexual and Domestic Violence
Office: (402) 476-6256

Website: **https://www.nebraskacoalitio n.org/**
Nevada Coalition to End Domestic and Sexual Violence
Office: (775) 828-1115

Website: **https://www.ncedsv.org/**
New Hampshire Coalition Against Domestic & Sexual Violence
Hotline: 1 (866) 644-3574

Website: **www.nhcadsv.org**

New Jersey Coalition to End Domestic Violence
Hotline: 1 (800) 572-7233

Website: **https://www.njcedv.org/**
New Mexico Coalition Against Domestic Violence
Office: (505) 246-9240

Email: info@nmcadv.org

Website: **www.nmcadv.org**
New York State Coalition Against Domestic
Violence
Hotline NYS: 1 (800) 942-6906

Hotline NYC: 1 (800) 621-4673

Website: **www.nyscadv.org**
North Carolina Coalition Against Domestic
Violence
Office: (919) 956-9124

Website: **www.nccadv.org**
CAWS North Dakota
Office: (701) 255-6240

Ohio Domestic Violence Network
Hotline: (800) 934-9840

Website: **www.odvn.org**
Oklahoma Coalition Against Domestic Violence &
Sexual Assault

Hotline: 1 (800) 522-7233

Email: info@ocadvsa.org

Website: **www.ocadvsa.org**
Oregon Coalition Against Domestic & Sexual Violence
Hotline: 1 (888) 235-5333

Website: **www.ocadsv.org**
Pennsylvania Coalition Against Domestic Violence
Office: (717) 545-6400

Website: **www.pcadv.org**
Coordinadora Paz para la Mujer (Puerto Rico)
Office: (787) 281-7579

Email: pplmsmtp@ayustar.net

Website: **www.pazparalamujer.org**
Rhode Island Coalition Against Domestic Violence
Hotline: 1 (800) 494-8100

Email: ricadv@ricadv.org

Website: **www.ricadv.org**
South Carolina Coalition Against Domestic Violence & Sexual Assault
Office: (803) 256-2900

Website: **www.sccadvasa.org**

South Dakota Coalition Ending Domestic Violence
& Sexual Assault
   Office: (605) 945-0869

   Website: **www.sdcedsv.org**
Tennessee Coalition To End Domestic & Sexual
Violence
   Hotline: 1 (800) 356-6767

   Website: **tncoalition.org**
Texas Council on Family Violence
   Office: (512) 794-1133

   Website: **www.tcfv.org**
Women's Coalition of St. Croix
   Hotline: (340) 773-9272

   Website: **https://wcstx.org/**
Utah Domestic Violence Coalition
   Hotline: 1 (800) 897-5465

   Website: **www.udvc.org**
Vermont Network Against Domestic & Sexual
Violence
   Hotline: 1 (800) 228-7395

   Website: **www.vtnetwork.org**
Virginia Sexual & Domestic Violence Action
Alliance
   Office: (804) 377-0335

Website: **www.vsdvalliance.org**
Washington State Coalition Against Domestic Violence
Hotline: 1 (800) 562-6025

Website: **www.wscadv.org**
West Virginia Coalition Against Domestic Violence
Office: (304) 965-3552

Website: **www.wvcadv.org**
Wisconsin Coalition Against Domestic Violence
Office: (608) 255-0539

Website: **endabusewi.org**
Wyoming Coalition Against Domestic Violence &
Sexual Assault
Office: (307) 755-5481

Website: **www.wyomingdvsa.org**

The Author

Cheryl L Gebbie is primarily a child of the ONE TRUE LIVING GOD. I come as a daughter, sister, mom, grandmother, and great grandmother. I have my bachelor's degree from what was known as Cumberland College, now known as University of the Cumberlands. My degree is in Public Health Education and Social Work. I work as the assistant for the She Will Heal Ministry and the To Blessed 2 Be Stressed Ministries here in Knoxville TN. In the past I have worked as a Certified Nursing Assistant in many different settings from Skilled Nursing Facilities as well as Rehab units, Hospice Units, Behavioral Units and Alzheimer's Units. Recently I have been working with Clients in their home. Some that need just companionship, some that need hospice care and some that just need help with mobility. Throughout my life God has been there with me. To Guide me, Heal Me, Protect Me, and my confidant. I am who I am because of GOD, My mom Betty Sneed, My children Rebecca Smith, Joshua Gilliam, and Jennifer Gilliam. My grandkids Mackenzie Gilliam, Lee-Anna Gilliam, Christopher Smith, and Karina Gilliam. And my great grandchildren, Emberlyn, Jax, Rose-Lynn, Lily, and Sage. My niece Christy Fairlie and her husband Micheal and her children Brice and Caitlin, My father-in-law Carl Gebbie and late mother-in-law Sharon Gebbie, nieces Ashlyn Shavers with husband JT, Niece Lauren Ailor with husband Nolan, their children Grace and son Timothy, my niece Nalitha Drew and her to boys Tru and Trey and many other people I do not see very often and others that I have contact with weekly. I love each one of you to the moon and back.

In the Mighty Name of Jesus: Thank you God for allowing me to author this book and I pray it helps many understand the issue and to help others know where to turn to and how to get out.

23315482R00046